The Adventures of Ivy and Kimber

KIMBER SNYDER

The Adventures of Ivy and Kimber

iUniverse books may be ordered through booksellers or by contacting:

iUniverse
1663 Liberty Drive
Bloomington, IN 47403
www.iuniverse.com
1-800-Authors (1-800-288-4677)

ISBN: 978-1-5320-7500-1 (sc)
ISBN: 978-1-5320-7501-8 (e)

Library of Congress Control Number: 2019906736

Print information available on the last page.

iUniverse rev. date: 06/20/2019

The Adventures of Ivy and Kimber

KIMBER SNYDER

The Adventures of Ivy and Kimber

In memory of Lee E. Hovis,
loving grandfather

When Kimber was eight years old, she wanted a pony very badly. Her older brother, Mike, had a pony named Buster, and she helped take care of him. Each morning, they would bring hay and grain for Buster to eat. Then, after school, they would clean out Buster's stall. Kimber's mom and dad watched her helping her brother take care of Buster and saw that she was doing a great job. They finally decided that she could have a pony of her own.

Her mom and dad searched for a pony that would be safe for a little girl, and they finally found the perfect pony. She was a pinto pony, and her name was Ivy. She was blind in one eye, and her front legs were slightly bent. Kimber didn't care about any of that. She was just so happy to have a pony of her very own. Kimber rode Ivy every day. She brushed her, cleaned her stall, and carried buckets of water to her. She made sure that Ivy had lots of grain and hay to eat. They had so much fun together, and Ivy soon became Kimber's best friend.

As time went on, everyone noticed that Ivy seemed to be gaining a lot of weight. Kimber was so worried that something was wrong with her pony. Her mom and dad called the veterinarian, and he came to their home to check on Ivy.

To everyone's surprise, the veterinarian told them that Ivy was going to have a baby. That was why she was gaining so much weight. The doctor checked Ivy all over and told the family when he thought the foal would be born. Kimber took extra-special care of Ivy every day.

The time came for when the doctor said the baby would be born, but ... no baby. Every day Kimber would hurry home from school and run to the barn. But ... no baby.

So much time had gone by that Kimber had almost given up hope. Then one day she came home from school, ran to the barn, and got the best surprise ever. There standing beside Ivy was a tiny little foal. Kimber was so excited she ran up to the house to get her mom and dad. They all ran to the barn to make sure everything was okay.

The foal was healthy and as cute as a button. Kimber's dad asked her what she was going to name him, and Kimber replied, "Pokey."

Her dad said, "Pokey? Why would you name him Pokey?"

Kimber said, "Because it took so long for him to get here."

Everyone laughed. Her dad said, "Pokey it is."

That is how Kimber came to have not just one pony to love and take care of but *two*: Pokey and Ivy.

KIMBER SNYDER, currently a registered nurse, earned a bachelor's degree in nursing from Slippery Rock University. A mother of two and a grandmother of two, she's had a lifelong love of horses and enjoys riding them still today. Snyder lives in the country near Franklin, Pennsylvania, with two Yorkies, seven chickens, and three horses. This is her debut book.

Printed in the United States
By Bookmasters